What a treasure! In this single volume are four hundred and seventy-seven tanka written and published by the acknowledged master of the form, Sanford Goldstein, during his fascinating forty-year journey along the tanka road.

Goldstein's poetic voice, and some of his techniques, have inevitably changed and evolved in response to life events experienced over those long years of commitment to tanka. But always his poetry emanates from his own modest persona, radiating out to illuminate a broad spectrum of topics which include nature and human nature, Goldstein's second country, Japan, his personal histories, religion, theatre, art, literature, and his own tanka-writing practices.

Though he is a consummate poet, Goldstein's language is characterized by simplicity, clarity, warmth, and often a gentle humor, which invite the reader into his life at every stage of its journey.

This invitation by Goldstein, to share a lifetime's memories and interaction with his present, celebrated in tanka, is one to be accepted gratefully and wholeheartedly.

—Amelia Fielden, translator and poet, Australia

Four Decades

on

My Tanka Road

For Anita and George —
Such brave people
I admire so much. May
you look at a few of my
poems as a memory.

Love, Sandy
April 5, 2008
Lyndhurst, Ohio

Four Decades on My Tanka Road

The Tanka Collections
of Sanford Goldstein

Sanford Goldstein

Edited by Fran M. Witham

With a Preface by Patricia Prime

MODERN ENGLISH TANKA PRESS
BALTIMORE, MARYLAND
2007

THE UNEXAMINED LIFE IS NOT WORTH LIVING.
SOCRATES

MODERN ENGLISH TANKA PRESS
P.O. Box 43717
Baltimore, Maryland 21236 USA
www.modernenglishtankapress.com
publisher@modernenglishtankapress.com

Four Decades on My Tanka Road :
The Tanka Collections of Sanford Goldstein

Cover art, woodprint portrait of Sanford Goldstein, by Kazuaki Wakui.
Copyright © 2007 by Kazuaki Wakui. Used by permission.
Four graphics within *This Tanka Whirl* (entitled "Life and Death") and that
book's cover etching, "two small trees by a stream in moonlight," are also
by Kazuaki Wakui.
Copyright © 2001 by Kazuaki Wakui. Used by permission.
The MU calligraphy is used, courtesy of Sanford Goldstein.

Four Decades on My Tanka Road :
The Tanka Collections of Sanford Goldstein

Printed in the United States of America
2007

ISBN 978-0-6151-8005-2

publisher@modernenglishtankapress.com
www.modernenglishtankapress.com

Dedication

my three tanka
on the back seat—
David
Rachel
Lisa

Acknowledgement

again, Hamlet,
you haul me to your heart,
to your precious mouth,
and I feel even tanka
can scale the spectacular

e
p
i
g
r
a
p
h

forty years have passed

and still my ear remains

a soft carpet

on which others

dance their blues

CONTENTS

Preface

The tanka in *Four Decades on My Tanka Road* are an intrinsic part of Sanford Goldstein's long life. The present book contains work from Goldstein's six published collections beginning in 1977 and the final one published in 2005, although *This Tanka World* (1977) contained previously unpublished poems written during the 60s. Goldstein has been on his 'tanka road' for more than forty years, if one considers that he first became aware of Takuboku in 1962 or so. This makes his tanka road longer than half his lifetime. He began the co-translation of *Tangled Hair* with Professor Seishi Shinoda in 1964—it took five years to complete and wasn't published until 1971.

Goldstein has taught literature both in America and Japan, where he has resided on and off for 27 years. He has been a professor, a co-translator, collaborator, and was co-editor of the tanka journal *Five Lines Down* for two years. He was editor of the tanka anthology *Sixty Sunflowers* and contributed to the recently published *Modern English Tanka* anthologies. Goldstein also writes prose—articles, essays and criticism. He has studied Japanese for 54 years and is still trying to improve his hearing and speaking of the language. He has emphasized the importance of Japanese translations, but he started Japanese late, so he says it has been a struggle. His many translations of Japanese novels, short stories and tanka poets are co-translations. Writes Goldstein to me, "I could have done nothing without my Japanese co-translators."

The new collection celebrates his voice as it has changed over the years—eventually he was acknowledged as one of the founding fathers of English language tanka. The book is also a tribute to the poet's imagination, commitment and resourcefulness operating under personal and practical constraints to bring readers his luminous tanka, which may be seen as a distillation from the experience of a poet who has earned the distinction of being a recognized elder and mentor.

What are we to expect of a poet who has been writing tanka for over four decades, has gained public recognition and respect, is friend and mentor to numerous aspiring tanka poets, and who has been called 'The Father of English Tanka'? Might this identification become a barrier to a proper appreciation of his writing?

It doesn't, of course, as he is such a modest man. Reading Goldstein's tanka will soon dispel any expectations that his work is to be read mainly for its 'message'. Not that his tanka are in any way divorced from his public or private life and the causes of tanka he has striven for. The tanka reflect the struggles and disappointments, the joys and happiness of a long life, as well as the aims and ideals for tanka, that have marked Goldstein's writing.

All good writing begins with the self. The body and its major events—sexuality, marriage, children, illness and ageing— provide a central metaphor for *Four Decades on My Tanka Road.* The range of Goldstein's subjects provides broad opportunities: from personal stories, to film, art, literature, Japan, poems about the 'spilling' of his tanka, nature and human nature. The traditional Japanese form is open to admit story, personal relationships, family, the natural world, humanity and translations.

A major decision occurred in Goldstein's life when he decided to travel to Matsuyama on Shikoku Island to visit Masanobu Fukuoka, the famous Japanese man whose book on natural farming, *The One-Straw Revolution,* he carried with him. That trip led to the publication of his tanka sequence *At the Hut of the Small Mind.* Here we have a sense of dislocation in the fact of being a *gaijin*-foreigner and the relief the poet found in writing tanka: "on the way up / to the mountain hut / the Zen farmer / crushes / a tangerine pest". The tanka relates an experience Goldstein had that occurred just as he was walking up to the hall where he was to have his first interview with Masanobu Fukuoka, when he says, "I was worried by the action of the Zen farmer killing that pest."

Goldstein was a lecturer at Niigata University from 1953-55. He stayed only two years, so did not break from his culture, but found himself in a culture where the world was turned upside down. *This Tanka World* (1977) is a collection of poems going back to the sixties and up to the date of its publication in 1977. During this time Goldstein and his wife went to Stanford for a year to study Japanese after they left Japan on that first visit, and for his wife to complete her Master's degree in anthropology. He taught at Purdue University from 1956-1992 and retired from Purdue in 1992 because he was invited to teach at a new college in Japan. During these Purdue years he held a Fulbright to Nagasaki, 1959-1961, and he returned to Niigata in 1964-1966, 1972-74, 1980-82 and 1987-89, although still connected to Purdue. His wife's death occurred in 1972. Willingly he chose to break away from his United States homeland in 1993. Eventually, in 2002, he gained lifelong resident status from the Japanese government. This long period in Japan led to a spiritual breakage with American traditions and culture and an embracing of those of his adopted country. In the process, the scars of this breakage are visible in his tanka, as one can see in the following tanka: "aboard the Sado Island ferry, / I too can stretch, / can pillow my head, / can tune-out a world / on these straw mats".

Goldstein uses simple language and makes direct statements, easy to understand, but profound feelings are there, too. A tanka in *This Tanka World* relates to his daughter: "my kid / glad / she'll be / the last / to die". The simplicity of style does not hide the poet's emotions. Many of his tanka are presented in a similar way, and we are left to draw our own conclusions. In his collection *Encounters in This Penny World,* he writes of his loss: "in the album / the dead one smiles while the kids / mimic a green ghost; / he tells his trio it's time / to get their bags, put on their masks".

The more one reads Goldstein, the more one feels the impact of this solitude that seems to permeate his poetic space in which "soundless / my return / and I light / the gas / to begin", "heater on / in this narrow room— / how shut out / again / this rough world", and "I pick up / the bowl / to drink / this self / in three's". If there is anything that lessens this sense of solitude, it is the writing of tanka: "this excuse for art / keeps me going: / I spill / what this fist / can't consume" and "day of cremation / and my three tanka / waiting wordless / in that

16

room /of Japanese mats". Here, the senses often blur boundaries between the individual and the collective body of the world. Many of Goldstein's poems are like this, short reflections about his own feelings, the problems he faces and the situations he is caught in. Others are of his experiences of childhood, education, marriage, retirement, old age and illness. Whether the poems speak from a personal or an impersonal perspective, they frequently use images from nature to describe passion. He is transformed by desire: "what brought on / the desire this time?— / something in last night's film? / a flicker on a bus? / a lamppost whimper?" Passion calls up a pure poetic surreality peppered with tales of humor, vitality and vigor. While the ageing body is perceived as "sick / for the very first time / in seventy years— / curious is he to discover / the physician's twists and turns".

Goldstein's love of literature often shows in his tanka. He writes of the book *Moby Dick*: "sharks / at those oars / driving a universe / into storms— / oh , Ishmael, what you saw, what experienced!" Ishmael had the power of language and the power to record and Goldstein's tanka also has some of that command of seeing and recording. Topics on art, literature, dance and theatre are never far from Goldstein's consciousness and help to form some of the stronger poems in the collection. He is never apologetic about writing on these matters, and always confident when asserting his identity as an 'outsider', living in Japan, or speaking about his Zen master: "the master / in black kimono sleeves, / sweeping skirt, / the back-row disciple knows / the eye cannot see itself". He attempts to touch the extreme limits of life with a language that carries with it the characteristics of simplicity, warmth, humor and emotion, as we see in a tanka from *This Tanka World* where his touching poem to his wife achieves the effects of empathy, love and devotion in a few simple lines: "rest / dear wife / from no-thought / from riddles of the universe / from the master's command". And he has achieved this amazingly well, building on a lifetime's experience and imagination to produce tanka of startling clarity, wit and wisdom. This is far from being the sum total of his tanka, for he writes eloquently about such things as the writing of his tanka, nature and the environment. But the core of his feeling remains firmly located in the 'spilling' of his five lines, a sentiment that is expressed in a number of poems. One of the finest of these may be the following tanka: "I came, / it seems, / to write solitary poems / in my Hut / of the Small Mind", where we see the poet alone, but not lonely, as he writes from his heart.

Sometimes Goldstein tries for the thirty-one syllable form in writing tanka: this may depend on the occasion. If he wants to show complete order a 31-syllable count helps. At other times he is content to deviate from the form to create his tanka using only a minimum of words. Using both the long and short forms of tanka has been easy for him to continue framing his poems over the years. In these simple lines he expresses the experiences of the personal and difficult moments of his life, as we see in the following minimalist poem: "I turn / the bowl / as told: / I drink / the analysis".

There is a marked change in Goldstein's collections over his forty or more years of writing tanka. Each collection is different, and I'd like to focus on a poem from one of his earlier works, *Gaijin Aesthetics* (whose title, I assume, is an ironic comment on the feeling of being an outsider, whether or not the poet is in Japan): "startled / this October / a.m.— / a bush / rising". In this tanka Goldstein practices constraint with his use of simplicity, using only seven words to convey his message. By contrast, in the final collection there is quite a change in terms of the form of the tanka. As well as 'the voice', he is concerned with the verse 'line'. This can be seen in the technique of the 'wrap around' line in some of the tanka in *Encounters in This Penny World*: "he refused the fray, / refused the circle's finite points / and stayed safe; / now he recalls the stages / where steps faltered, staggered, slowed". The overflow of sentence to pause mid-poem and the frequency of punctuation and repetition are a characteristic method of breaking up a long line into units that are easier to comprehend. This is not a consistent pattern in the volume and there are constant variations, which are closely allied to his growing interest in story telling. In another poem in this collection he writes: "thirty years of zazen, / and satori not in sight, / he closets his pillow: / it will be there tomorrow / for his early morning routine", where he uses a generative line that pushes itself forward so that the poet can forget about it and tell his story.

The collection *At the Hut of the Small Mind* is one of Goldstein's contributions towards the definition of a tanka sequence. He defines in an essay at the beginning of the book what a tanka sequence is. He spent five years translating Mokichi Saitō's *Red Lights* and defined it there with Professor Shinoda. All the sections in *Red Lights* are tanka sequences, and in the notes Professor Shinoda and Goldstein pointed out why they were. So *At the Hut of the Small Mind* is what he considers a tanka sequence, perhaps the longest written in English. At the end of

a tanka sequence there is a change in the poet or the poet's view
of the world. You do not have to say what that change was, but
it occurs in several poems before the 'I' actually leaves. As an
example from this outstanding work I quote two tanka: one
from the beginning and one towards the conclusion to illustrate
this growth and development in the persona:

> I toss out
> a theory
> in this Zen hut,
> but how real
> the brown rice ball in my hand

and

> I shave away
> my do-nothing life,
> all the dampness
> unfolded and left out to dry,
> and still: that solidity on my shoes

Goldstein has a modest, self-effacing voice. This does not
diminish the poetry but is indicative of the precise balance with
which he regards life—from his children, to his students, to
retirement and to the ageing process. The ability to take a fist
full of words and in a very short space transform it is a
wonderful gift. Goldstein also has the ability to attribute exact
measures—the exact measure of language to the requisite
thought or emotion. His lyrics move fluidly, illuminating each
conflict or predicament. His control extends not only to his

words but also to the space that he allows around them. He is master of permitting the unsaid to more than complement the actuality expressed: of following each nuance of thought, indicating each hesitation in approaching a perplexity simply through punctuation, lineation and breaks.

There is plenty here for the attentive reader. A lifetime's memories move with the present in the poet's consciousness, richly freighting the tanka's formal minimalism, blending human loves and griefs, physicality and spirituality, into a superb whole.

— *Patricia Prime*
Auckland, New Zealand
November 2007

Four Decades on My Tanka Road

Part I

This Tanka World

1977

Four Decades on My Tanka Road

Sanford Goldstein

all I saw
was the hole
in my kid's
sock
when she performed

        my kid
        glad
        she'll be
        the last
        to die

            said
            that wet spot
            in her bed
            was last night's
            rain

                  of
                  kids
                  and
                  mates
                  mothers
                  and
                  dads

like an assassin
I too
aim for the head
striking
my kid

my own harsh way
and still
still
this affection
for my kids

never thought
Buddha
could sew
until my wife's
evening fingers

my three tanka
on the back seat—
David
Rachel
Lisa

calm
as Buddha
she stoops
and wipes
the blood away

                  suddenly
                  my mother's
                  tears
                  remembering
                  her dad

all my rebellion
gone
with this haircut
my wife
gave me

my kid
says
she wants to watch
Laura
and Hearty

a glance
from my kid
hoping the old man
won't see
her television tears

unable
to embrace
the shoulders
of my wrestling
son

cafeteria
morning:
coffee cups
and spoons
and talk

as if life
will settle
it all
I drink my coffee
write my poem

home from coffee
I climb
the stairs
to see
if they're all right

of
coffee
cups
and
tables

once more
the day's cycle:
poems
over the coffee cup
and this spring rain

black coffee
and this dark
September rain
darkening
the green

on my way
for coffee
I recite
yesterday's
poem

Friday night
in this lonely
conference town
I drink coffee
under a dim light

so quiet
this coffee
morning
even this pen
this spoon

thick February flakes
beyond
the cafeteria pane
I want to steep this cup
in dreams

over the coffee cup
this April day
all the old demons
march
out

this cafeteria self
I see
sitting
waiting
for some poem to eat

even
in this fourth
wifeless summer
I take my coffee
with cream

in this corner
booth
I write
my poem
the first of June

ash
from the incense stick
falls
quietly
this summer day

when I was a kid
it was punks
now
it's incense
in the master's room

dusty
incense sticks
deep
inside
this drawer

of
zen
and
the
master

———

I look
at the MU
of Hoseki
unable to find
my self

reminded
again
of impermanence—
how thick this Sunday morning
snow

I bite down
hard
on this March
zen
world

Sanford Goldstein

this February
light
lengthens
the day wrapped
in a cloth of cranes

his Japanese delicacy
a coarse tightrope
sweetness
between chrysanthemum
and sword

the bars of candy
I gave him
for the bus
he'll devour them
too

where
was
no-thought
when
the crisis came?

even
the master's
sleeve
an endless
cul-de-sac

his words
of farewell
written
on the fan
I use this fall day

no clasping of hands
no clichés
we stand and bow
by the bus
this summer day

stripped
jabbed
wiped—
my wife
on a hospital bed

behind
those thick frames
her old man
holds back
a flood

my wife's
cut hair
given
in a brown hospital bag
by the cashier

of
sickness
and
hospitals
life
and
death

in this narrow
hospital room
my wife
stares
at the falling rain

summer gone
and all that pain
of surgery
and after
slides into a niche

rest
dear wife
from no-thought
from riddles of the universe
from the master's command

that umbilical
they coiled
and gave us
in a pretty Japanese box—
where is it now?

now I know
life and death
sit back-to-back
my kid four on the fourth
my dad dead on the fifth

planting
a white
chrysanthemum
in the hair
of the dead one

the entire world
shifting
sinking
I open windows in the morning
close them at night

Tamura out into the sea
Mishima with a sword
and others I could name with pills—
tonight
I count these ways of dying

strangely quiet
seeing a man die
last night live
on tv
strangely quiet today

midnight
insomniac
trying to shove
time
under this Japanese quilt

I watch
a purple coat
walking
a bearded jaw
talking

something
lonely
about an umbrella in rain
two legs
moving

carried
my loneliness
home
in a brown
paper bag

of
things

45

the pile
of leaves
raked Sunday
still a pile
today

something gaunt
and lonely
by the early morning
bus stop
snow

along the alley
this winter evening
garbage cans
stand empty
without lids

again
this catalogue
of past griefs
and I keep washing
the same dish

look
to see
if I'm zipped
after
tucking it in

so much
poverty
misery
in this elevator
up to the desired floor

the white wall
I painted
this morning
whiter
at midnight

cold night
and all
the living room
pictures
crooked

lonely
their shuffle
of kitchen cards
this October
night

on the living room wall
the stick the master gave me:
whether said
or not
thirty strokes

at the distant end
of this narrow street
a sun
more red
than holocaust

ready
in this new
December tie
to confront
the fifth decade

each footstep
shakes
that yellow ball
over these campus
trees

want to walk
this spring day
and turn desire
on a spit
until it's done

I wait
like a breath held
for something to happen
these rain-drenched
summer days

of
strangers
loners
and
outside
persons

wifeless
in front
of a white stove
after a 5:30
class

shibui
wabi
sabi
and some temple bell
in this mind

when will I
unplug these ears
and hear
sirens
along the coast?

this summer night
at the magazine rack
fingers
desperately
turning

that blue sky
no arrow
can pierce
I lie on my summer back
punching, mauling

was it
two rejections
or three?—
though these were only
by mail

September midnight
and I want
the bare
suchness
of *now*

no causes to uphold
I pen
these lines
over a fragile cup
this summer day

loneliness
piles up
at midnight
and sometimes
spills over

even at midnight
this run-around
mask
never
falls off

the voice of my kid
wakes me
rolling over
I feel
the morning of my wife

lighting
the memorial candle
for my wife
I put it
on a white plate

at night
turbulent dreams
in this wifeless
winter
bed

of
sex
and
love
and
marriage

endless
this passionless
day
this passionless
night

all night
as if this skin
splattered
with oil
in crucial places

outside
the kitchen door
I hear
a dog whine
waiting to mount our mutt

this niche
for sperm
overflows
these fall
days

lying in bed
after
I see
the moon
through this summer screen

closed
my eyes
at midnight
opened them
at dawn

driving for coffee
after the film
my wife and I
silent
looking through rain

that young skin
should not be
this fresh
in the December
light

tonight
everyone seems endowed
under
this thick
January moon

Sanford Goldstein

again today
I tease anguish
into fixing lunch
poring down a page
and laughing over the phone

                            nowadays
                            the quiet walk
                            up to my room
                            the quiet entry
                            to bed

to love
to be loved
either or both
this last midnight
of the year

59

this thick emptiness
wraps
round me
in the Florida
light

they ask
about the cooking
cleaning, kids
of midnight
not a word

nothing
transcendent
this spring day
of soft
spring rain

of
various
kinds
of
nothingness

Sanford Goldstein

cold today
and wind
slowly snow
settles
on a black tree

the niche
I've found
hardly
room enough
for me

last night
I took out
the master's
nothingness
for this bare wall

again and again
corridor smiles
and the old nausea
wets
my blue shirt

and now
another summer
looms
before these scant
hands

nothing
to do
in this February world
nothing
to be

what's
this emptiness
in the hanging scroll
the master
gave me?

my loss of freedom?
a curved line
skirting
the edge
of *now*

tonight
I feel
her nausea
for this penny
world

this afternoon
emptiness
stays and stays
outside there's snow
and the face of another

home
to this emptiness
and upstairs
more
of the same

again
today
nothing
satisfied
me

eating temple cookies
I walk round
and behind
until I find a chair
marked wallflower

        how these scattered
        bits of salad
        color
        this November
        world

    walked
    forty minutes
    for a bowl of soup
    walked
    forty minutes back

           of
           food

scolding
the kids
at lunch
got egg
on my shirt

even my youngest
knows
something's wrong
cleaned up
her plate

in a sweat
I devour my meal
let a fork drop
and I pummel
the world

cardinal red
in the February snow
I scatter
pellets of bread
hoping to stop some mad flight

in some distant
kitchen
this November night
I see hands
making

this soft ball
of rice
at the end of these sticks
memories
of Japan

spoon
over the frying pan
browning
and spilling
thought

put on a record
for lunch
fry some rice
and sit
at this winter table

I remain
in this *about* world
afraid to suck
the core
of *now*

Sanford Goldstein

called
a poet
once on Monday
once
on Thursday

like
the bourgeois
gentilhomme
didn't know
it was tanka

no gravel
in these lines
yet how rough
the music
on my tongue

*of
tanka*

69

this very air
tanka
no rhythm of 31
no word-juggle
only the deep of *now*

having played
at poems
find
there's no faking it
tonight

a decade
of painful
moments
in this fistful
of poems

on
first
looking
into Takuboku's
tanka!

Akiko
my teacher
and Takuboku too
whose pain
I hang in these lines

in zen
a direct-pointing-to
in tanka
I *this*
the world

striving
for 31
find the form
explodes
in my face

this life
a cutting of paper forms
pasted
in scraps
and bits

lamp glow
on my desk
ledger
open
for poems

Sanford Goldstein

let the print
be darkest black
the paper coarse
the rough edge
cut this flesh

want
to cram
this moment
into a tanka
fist

sick
of pretty
haiku
on a pretty
page

these tanka
fold, bend
like *origami*
cranes
under this hand

Postscript to *This Tanka World*

'this very air/tanka/no rhythm of 31/no word-juggle/only the
deep of *now*'—so goes one of my tanka, that form of Japanese
poetry 1200 years old yet only brought back to life in this
century through the efforts of Akiko Yosano (1878-1942) and
Takuboku Ishikawa (1886-1912). Akiko's *Tangled Hair* prepared
me for tanka as love, Takuboku's *Sad Toys* for the broader
spectrum of all man's activities. I think of myself, though, as
Takubokian. It was Takuboku who brought tanka closest to
colloquial language while still guarding its poetic element,
Takuboku who said that the tanka need not restrict itself to
thirty-one syllables, Takuboku who taught me that tanka is a
diary of the emotional changes in a man's life. I feel my own
tanka are non-confessional diary, and I am supported in this
belief by one of my colleagues who calls my five-liners utterly
personal and intimate yet perfectly public. He calls my language
the most commonplace, the poems capable of being written by
anyone. I regard this as lovely praise.

—Sanford Goldstein

Four Decades on My Tanka Road

Part II

Gaijin Aesthetics

1983

for/ the dead one,
long sleeves,
my three tanka
on a back seat,
and Neil

Preface to *Gaijin Aesthetics*

For sixteen years I have been a writer of tanka, that Japanese poetic form traditionally spilled in one line and divided into syllables of 5-7-5-7-7. And for twenty-eight years I have been connected to Japan, whether living on her shores or in America. The Japanese dub foreigners outsiders, *gaijin* (literally: outside persons), pronounced *guy-gene*. But whether I am in Japan or not, the feeling of outsiderdom persists—walking along the Niigata seashore or sitting at a tea ceremony or sharing a lonely Saturday night treat with my shadow or moving along a corridor after an unsuccessful class.

My own foreign-brand of tanka is spontaneous, though occasionally re-ordered, re-shaped, and yet the desire persists that, like a line out of a Western poem, my own single line will spring fully armed from the head of Zeus. My tanka are molecules bouncing against one another, each tanka a separate entity even while sometimes splitting the previous tanka or joining it or leaping over others to join or attack or partially split. Whether above or below, inside or outside, in Japan or not, in them, in my tanka world, I feel an aesthetic, a line connected and disconnected, ordered and broken, but with a rhythm and color and touch lighting up the commonplace world of *sabi* or *wabi*, past or present, darkness or dawn, a host of cascading opposites.

And so these *gaijin* tanka, these *gaijin* aesthetics . . .

> Sanford Goldstein
> Niigata, Japan
> October 1981

muse
that inspires
gaijin
on these isolate shores,
let these tanka pour

this excuse for art
keeps me going:
I spill
what this fist
can't consume

pretty haiku
again
on pretty pages—
I want to cut a belly
five spaces thick

where's the depth
in these five lines down?—
I walk
a seaside road
I talk to self

Basho,
your umbilical cord
connection
and, yes,
your frog

leaping
even out of a clerk's
mouth:
this evening's
tanka

it's a narrow
way
full of commonplace
ruts—
this tanka world

I'm vulnerable
to the pulled sleeve
along ancient corridors—
oh, Murasaki,
sing your songs to me

Sanford Goldstein

in the bicycle basket
the crone
pushed up
the slope—
tonight's flower arrangement

how bright
the runner's headband
along this seaside road—
Mishima!
Mishima!

85

funny
hearing it
called
The Year
of the Cock

outside
and sitting
in this slight
end-of-July rain,
an ancient in cotton robes

single stars
over this Sea of Japan
and I want
to make them lonely
too

Butterfly,
you seem to stand
eternally
before that paper-covered door
looking through holes in the universe

I carry
the garbage bag
to the dump site—
early August rain
and a brushstroke wind

no wind
over this September
sea
only the cry
of a stray

Sanford Goldstein

startled
this October
a.m.—
a bush
rising

he crops up
every then
and then—
that Master
of Zen

somewhere
not even body
or mind
to drop
off

was it this morning's
fog-loneliness
made that hump
in the back
of the seaside Toyota?

soundless
my return
and I light
the gas
to begin

lunchtime
and the soliloquy
settles
over rice
over sugarless tea

heater on
in this narrow room—
how shut out
again
this rough world

another box
handed me
at the door—
I shall turn sweet
before the end of the year

in my element?
a Saturday night wind
and solitary
farts
before the set

it's Sunday
under this vast sky
and I oriental-walk
as if there's someplace to go
something to do

suddenly
caught:
the emptiness
in that girl's
yawn

in cold palms
how sweet
last night's
coffee
mug

at last
night's passing
I pick up my bed
I boil water
for tea

I breathe
in and out
I sweep
I dust
I tomorrow

Saturday night:
sounds of this pen,
the washing machine,
and my kid
yawning over the Constitution

trying
to tune
tonight's alone,
I butter
a roll

to fill
that wetness
with solidity—
tonight's
distant desire

rained-on
this umbrella-less
day,
I huddle
the bus-stop sign

she waters
the gravestone
this day
the dead
return

a long tunneled
view
from tomorrow's
slope
and all the *empty*

she came
bringing the gift
of a worried face—
my kid ill
on a hospital bed

slowly
the world thinned out
along hospital corridors
and I was left
with my kid

a winter
huddling
against heaters
against socks
against the prick of wool

under
thick counterpanes
the empty
accessibility
of tonight's world

Sanford Goldstein

snow
piling
a crane's wing
wings across
this bare mind

I pick up
the bowl
to drink
this self
in three's

the curve
in this tea ceremony
flower
tells me what's wrong
with my penny world

tonight's
Van Gogh
shoes
damp through
by the kitchen door

it chose
an arm
covered with wool,
that pup,
for its three-second hump

as if she knows
this vegetable kingdom
the Geisha madame
selecting
tonight's stew

wild goose
across
a chestnut moon:
I eat this sweet
before the bitter tea

as if the miracle's
poised
at elbow—
this morning cry
liking my life

the afternoon loneliness
grabs me
and I boil water
and break open
the delight

I turn
the bowl
as told:
I drink
the analysis

something
silk and cold
falling
falling
on tonight's *gaijin*

the balcony moon
caving in, in,
and darkening
tonight's
exclusion

how the mood
takes over—
a button-shop memory
where once the dead one
bowed

there are secrets
still
to be kept
in this night-soil
world

Sanford Goldstein

Part III

At the Hut of the Small Mind
A Tanka Sequence

1992

Four Decades on My Tanka Road

Introduction to
At the Hut of the Small Mind

In July 1982, I traveled to Matsuyama on Shikoku Island to visit the nearby farm of Masanobu Fukuoka, the famous Japanese farmer whose book on natural farming, *The One-Straw Revolution*, I carried with me. An editor of a small American press had asked me to interview Mr. Fukuoka. I knew a little about Mr. Fukuoka's Zen experience, and since I had been interested in Zen Buddhism for at least twenty years and since a Zen master had lived in my house in Indiana on two separate occasions of a year each, I went to Shikoku with trepidation---I would be courting difficulties and the inevitable contradictions that surface in any Zen-oriented world.

Since my spoken Japanese succeeds only on the most mundane levels, I planned my list of some twenty-eight or so questions, planned them with the help of two Japanese friends in Niigata, where I had been living and teaching the past two years. That list I no longer have, for Mr. Fukuoka confiscated it without my ever getting beyond the first question, which he claimed had to be answered before any of the others could be. That question concerned itself with *satori*, or enlightenment, and since my own little breakdown of the written Japanese character for *satori* included five mouths in order to explain the emotion behind *satori*, I was aware of the difficulties I would be encountering by posing that question first. A young Japanese who was at the farm to learn Mr. Fukuoka's methods of Japanese farming and perhaps to translate Mr. Fukuoka's latest book into English (I was never quite certain) sat by me to pass on in English the various statements made by Mr. Fukuoka.

Those three nights and four days I spent at Matsuyama remain memorable—days that were among the most difficult I had spent on my five two-year trips to Japan during the last thirty-two years. It was a period in which I felt I was throwing off much of the clutter (and ease) of the modern world. I was of course frightened and frustrated, and yet I realized I was in the middle of something crucial to life, my own and that of other persons, something ambiguous and beckoning and building. My bare cabin without electricity or running water with an easy accessibility to all that crawls or flies in the outside world, my keyless door and battered screens, my pile of damp *futon*—all that found me groping in darkness after a long first-night session with the farmer and some family members and neighbors and disciples. I was obviously the *gaijin*-foreigner who had come to ask questions, not someone there to work at natural farming.

Later I helped with meals, with cleaning the kitchen floor and low table we ate at, with sweeping and peeling. It was not the KP of my remote life back in the forties. Throughout I felt something of *mu* (interpreted audaciously as I write this introduction as Buddhism's complex yet rich nothingness), of *sabi* (acceptable human loneliness), of *wabi* (the preciousness of old things in all their bare limitations). I remember feeling that even Matsuyama's hills were *wabi*, an obvious poetic-license-*ism*. There were natural peaches, natural rice fields, natural tangerines, and natural summer-*mikan* (unlike anything tangerine in the world with their *shibui* rough-textured shapes and skins), and of course the world was *shiori*, effectively and variously ambiguous on several different levels.

I had come to interview, but only occasionally did I meet Mr. Fukuoka, who appeared and disappeared with strange regularity. I thought he had given me more attention than I deserved in that long three-hour nighttime session in which I had felt like something out of Breughel watched by more than twenty-four eyes. My interviewless-interview found me less a questioner than an examiner of this American self sometimes defecating in a shed under rains that seemed to proclaim some antediluvian connection. But if I saw less of my famous Zen farmer, I saw more of Rebecca, an American from the East Coast studying natural farming, yet more concerned, I felt, with trying to find the Zen way, the Gateless Gate, the magic formula that somehow allows one to walk this tightrope life without falling down. There was also that young Japanese translator (Jiro I shall call him) who every now and then sat poring over Japanese texts. It was odd the third day out to be invited by a group of four young workers, including Rebecca and Jiro, to spend a long rain-filled afternoon and long long evening together, the first at a famous Japanese hot spring bath on the island and then, as if to reinforce the irrationalities of my journey, at a disco bar.

I was actually torn between staying longer at the farm or spending a full week in Kyoto as I had originally planned. But another American visitor suddenly arrived to help me decide to leave. Late in the morning of my fourth day I walked the long muddy road down to a spot where taxis maneuvered along the highway to the airport.

I had no advance plan to write *At the Hut of the Small Mind*, but I had, ever since 1964, kept up what I call my tanka diary. Since I have almost never counted out the traditional thirty-one syllables in writing my tanka poems, it has been easy to continue framing tanka over the years, yet it has always been hard to come up with a good one. At any rate, I knew in advance that I'd be adding poems to my tanka diary, but I hadn't expected to be so on my own in the hut I lived in. I had never before so vividly experienced the limits of my own quite limited self.

And so this tanka sequence: *At the Hut of the Small Mind*. For quite a long long time, more than a decade in fact, I had thought I was writing tanka sequences, but actually I was writing clusters of poems around a single event or experience or person or thought or feeling. It is not my intention to discount those earlier efforts. But for the last five years I had been studying and translating Mokichi Saitō's *Shakkō* (*Red Lights*) with my long-time tanka-translator-collaborator, Professor Seishi Shinoda, and it was through our joint study that I came to realize the dramatic impact of a tanka sequence with its beginning, middle, and end toward some new awareness of the self and/or the world. Mokichi's dramatic night-run entitled "Sad Tidings," the run made just after he learned of the death of his famous teacher Sachio Itō, is perhaps the most famous tanka sequence in Japanese---unless it is Mokichi's sequence on the death of his mother. Whether or not my own tanka sequence is perhaps the first tanka sequence in English by a foreigner is of little consequence, but that it is at least a true tanka sequence pleases me, consisting as it does of the day before my trip to Shikoku, the trip to Matsuyama, the four-day stay at the farm, and the following twenty-four hours in Kyoto.

Perhaps a note of clarification is in order: Mr. Fukuoka calls his method of farming do-nothing farming. While this is misleading since a great deal of labor does go into his methods, I believe he means by it his protest against the excessive procedures modern farmers are forced into complying with for their yields. A devoted advocate of natural farming, Mr. Fukuoka has gained the admiration of a large following.

Sanford Goldstein
West Lafayette, Indiana
December 1985

Four Decades on My Tanka Road

devouring
these supermarket cakes
as if tomorrow's
trip
may be my last!

    wanting
    tonight's
    window gaze
    an almost-*satori*—
    and still only this neon, only this car glare

I pass rice fields,
tiled roofs,
pine, and all the rest;
oh, Japan,
my passing is a passing through

a taxi maze
among
these Matsuyama hills—
until at last
the farm! the farm!

in his rubber raincoat
stark
against white hair
and drooping specs,
the solidity of master?

    on the way up
    to the mountain hut
    the Zen farmer
    crushes
    a tangerine pest

        they give me
        food—
        I eat
        napkinless,
        chopsticks without Japanese points

through
this candle-
glow
the eyes
of my natural farmer

around the table
of this mountain hut
our Zen farmer
talking his way
through *mu*

I toss out
a theory
in this Zen hut,
but how real
the brown rice ball in my hand

Sanford Goldstein

I zigzag
my way
through theoretical Zen,
hurling my smile
at the master's face

first night:
in the dark
I stumble for a place
to send my urine
natural

how many before me
have found in this mountain hut
moths clinging to corners,
mosquitoes
over this July flesh?

how bare
this mountain hut,
my unwashed body
reduced
to summer smell

    voices distant
    from my mountain hut
    and the long long
    cry
    of falling rain

        the flesh clings
        tighter still
        as if to tell me
        this world is smell,
        is touch

a universe
of crawling, flying,
sounding
ambiguities:
insomnia in my mountain hut

that wing
brushed
by candleflame,
and still it fluttered,
still it flew

I am a lump
of thought
this fragmented night
of insect cry
and crawl

I listen
for the soundless—
oh, you analyst,
can't you hear?
can't you smell?

I too
am Basho,
fleas
and that urine smell
in this mountain hut

up this mountain
I came
with my usual
bag
of dishrag servilities

in a corner
tacked
to the mud wall
of my mountain hut,
Mother Teresa

it was roosters
at morning light-fall—
how joyous
even that crack
diagonal

is it
with rain water
I wash?
first morning
in these Matsuyama hills

outside
my hut
where I piss,
am I stepping on radish,
on burdock?

it's by candlelight
and perpetual
cock-crow
I write
my morning poem

in the morning's
candlelight glimmer,
I sweep
these mountain hut
mats

no god
came down
to tap my shoulder,
to say
there's a primitive world

the master
gathers the young,
and by candlelight
dissects
their various worlds

chickens
with legs
on solid ground:
this morning world
at my Matsuyama hut

is it coffee
withdrawal
giving me
this huge split
at the back of my skull?

Sanford Goldstein

in this Hut
of the Small Mind,
I'm made
to read
about "knowing"

    why I came:
    the Zen farmer
    asks twice,
    three times,
    as if my own koan's in it

where's the talk
at breakfast
poking these chopsticks
into *miso* soup,
vegetables, rice?

the others
my Zen farmer led
to practicalities,
me to abstractions
in the Hut of the Small Mind

sounds
of labor in those fields,
sounds
of insect cry,
and, of course, cock-crow

how vivid
that spider
in its lair
I urinate
by

at least
Mother Teresa
smiles at me
from the mud wall
in my Hut of the Small Mind

for hours
I lay
on my hut *futon*
till
even the candleglow waned

as if the world
out there
not nature enough,
a picture of a bird
nailed to my hut's wall

I walk
to the natural rice fields
and back,
I write
my natural poem

green and more green
and greener
still,
these tangerine leaves
in the July rain

the cool
of rain,
July relief
in my Hut
of the Small Mind

not a single complaint
do I hear
from these blades of grass
bombarded
by afternoon rain

all day
in this hut,
mind poring
over the abstract prose
of this man of Zen

       a mountain child
       in this Hut
       of the Small Mind,
       I wrap the dampness
       round

          that bee
          stayed and stayed
          as if it too
          sought shelter
          from the July flood

the hills
are *wabi*,
and there's a *shiori* smell
in this Hut
of the Small Mind

communal chopsticks,
and the tips
they mouth
poked into pickles
noodles, rice

the daylight's
long in its descent;
it's by gray shadow
I write
my pre-candle poem

ugly
as facial scars
this *natural* summer-tangerine,
and how bitter
on my tongue!

it might be
Rembrandt:
candleglow shadow
and a student
over his text

only English
spoken round
the mountain hut table—
oh, how silent
is my Japanese

into peyote, he tells me,
and all the rest,
that huddled Japanese
translating the master's
mu

dear Rebecca,
cursing your own people,
you'll never Zen
the long, the lonely
road

from communal vegetables
and rice,
how solitary
the wet night walk
back to my mountain hut

gaining
at least
a two-day growth
of beard
in my Hut of the Small Mind

clutching
bank kleenex
as I squat:
I hear rain slanting
against the shed

I came,
it seems,
to write solitary poems
in my Hut
of the Small Mind

these burly
summer-*mikan*
might be sumo wrestlers
waiting
at ringside

do these pine-tree cutters
on their trees
before the noodle shop
sometimes look at these Matsuyama hills,
these fields of rice?

Sōseki,
you came to these
Matsuyama hills,
chucking away
careers

it's *wabi*
of course:
the old tangerine
crate
against the hut's mud wall

modern civilization?
a black butterfly
in from the rain
through my mountain hut's
battered door

eating
the peach,
I wonder
how natural
it is

this natural
peach
with its natural color
and natural worm,
can I suck it natural?

eating my peach
in the quiet rain,
I listen
to the master's
verse

how minute
the complexities
of even this small world
round
the morning meal

with a rag
I wipe the kitchen floor
wood;
and with a rag
I wipe it again

one sharp verbal blow
from the master
straight at the bull's-eye
of her desire:
Rebecca's tears

this rice bowl
I hold
in the rain—
oh, I want to rinse
after the floss!

    back
    propped against a wall:
    I prepare
    to listen
    to light

        same meal,
        same faces,
        same chopstick plunge,
        and still, still,
        this mountain hut life

no waiting
for guests
or for love
at my Hut
of the Small Mind

a motley crew,
some bearded, some in battered
work-a-day clothes,
we make our own way
from these mountain huts

at last
at the public bath
a public back wash
and my hot spring
soak!

how multiple
the uses of my mountain
towel,
sometimes for washing,
sometimes for rain

lolling
in their genital
towels,
these hot spring
discussants

it was
a day
of stories by the young
of their troubled
trips

on the disco
floor
in the armless arms
of the young,
I remember other backs, other faces

they are young
and young and young,
their mountain farm energy
even in their dappled
disco dance

how they peered
at the disco bill
until "grandpa"
pulled out
a ten thousand

told
I'll be a good gramp:
it's not
with much delight
I look at Rebecca's young face

nothing
to catch, to clutch,
though I extend
my hand
this disco night

it's in pouring
rain
I stick out my thumb
to bum
a midnight ride to my hut

again
clutching bank kleenex,
I squat—
was it ages ago
I foretold Buddha's shitstick?

at Natural Farm
is it all futile,
this attempt
to let it all
hang out?

my body
unmasks
in candleglow
the rain
down down

trying to make up
my *Namu Amida Butsu's*
on these missed mountain nights,
I give the dead one
several extras

interfering rain,
how will I make
that slippery way
down the mud
with my tomorrow bag?

a drenched chicken
pecking
at splashes
before the mountain hut
kitchen

woodgathering
in rain,
Rebecca in her blue poncho:
I have scribbled
my morning poem

    my chopsticks
    dig
    into the communal salad:
    final breakfast
    at Do Nothing Farm

      I taste
      this potato
      in gruel;
      I savor the salt
      in this pickled plum

at the master's
feet,
two Americans,
one Japanese,
and a white hen

like
a Don Quixote
with a Chinese beard,
the master came,
the master went away

like masters
of Zen,
appearing, disappearing:
three chickens
at Do Nothing Farm

that mud
on your nose,
Rebecca,
tells me
this world is right

at the hot spring, Jiro,
you did not cover
your physical self,
but what you left covered, Jiro,
was immense

      urinating
      from my hut door,
      I too join
      this rain
      on green leaf

in this natural world
tears, sighs, blows,
all faded,
faded in the steady rain
on my hut

once,
seeing my smile
that did its silent work,
the master stopped
his word-flow

whether I stay
or don't,
whether I write
my article or let it pass,
I am in this Hut of the Small Mind

wanting to stay,
I could not,
and leaving,
I wanted
to write ten thousand poems

my interview-less
interview is over,
and bag in hand,
I descend
the muddy road

as if clutching
the master's
thirty-one,
I leave
Do Nothing Farm

no farewell
except
this calligraphy'd sheet,
I watch the master
trudge off in mountain rain

the balloon
he drew
with a brush
carries
all the nothingness away!

as if expelled
from further room
at the inn,
I leave
my Hut of the Small Mind

I see another
arrival
for his own three-day
as if a brief fondled *mu*
can be tucked away

in muddy trousers
and muddy shoes
I go down
the mud-filled road
from the Hut of the Small Mind

throat bearded,
I back into
the world
from Do Nothing
Farm

I drag down
the *sabi* emptiness
of my mountain hut;
in Kyoto
there's rain

Sanford Goldstein

changing
into another gyration
of self,
I return
to the everyday whirl

I shave away
my do-nothing life,
all the dampness
unfolded and left out to dry,
and still: that solidity on my shoes

away from
Do Nothing Farm,
and this rain-stilled
Kyoto night
is tender, is sad

the American
that took
my place,
is he watching
Rebecca's sad eyes?

    it rains
    on and on,
    and the mountain damp
    extends
    even to my Kyoto bath

        in a taxi
        along this Kyoto street,
        two hairstyles
        of sumo wrestlers
        from the back window . . .

Four Decades on My Tanka Road

Part IV

Records of a Well-Polished Satchel : . . . No. 7 14 Occasion Tanka

1995

Four Decades on My Tanka Road

1

mesmerized
by gazes left
and right,
I stand on this train,
a white chrysanthemum in my hand

2

how to muster will,
tie it tight
as if with bows
or rubberbands
and hold it in my grip

3

he is gone, gone,

my Zen master

with his mysterious sleeves,

his Giaconda smile,

his answer to that jumping eyeball he once showed

4

how vast
this edge of years
between 67 and 70:
tonight
I eat my meal with gusto

5

aboard the Sado Island ferry,
I too can stretch,
can pillow my head,
can tune-out a world
on these straw mats

6

I keep
my fence distance
and finally
the white
does not bark at me

7

I have used sandpaper
to smooth down
the rough edges of
forty years of pain—
I'm a gloss, I'm a précis

8

it was a day
of worming through language,
worming through crowds,
and still, once through a train window
cherry blossoms

9

a green worm crawling
along my morning walk
and in a mind-flash
my kid-stick
poking circles into a nether world

10

what brought on
the desire this time?—
something in last night's film?
a flicker on a bus?
a lamppost whimper?

Sanford Goldstein

11

it was as usual
a lonely bed performance
where the dancer
whirled through handclasp
and the shadows puppeted about

181

12

hushed
by today's monotony,
I need a Whitman
to lean against
over this spent cave of self

13

encamped now
in my new domain
I settle for less
I subordinate
I diminish

14

how set
this cylinder of rice
rolled with seaweed—
I bite into memory,
I samurai my coffee cup

Sanford Goldstein

Four Decades on My Tanka Road

Part V

This Tanka Whirl

2001

Sanford Goldstein

#1

somersault tanka

so tame,
so tame,
these tanka tribulations:
sometimes I want berserk music
for some world in me gone berserk!

can't remember
a wild leap
from my bed,
windows flung open,
and the out-there, the out-there!

at times, mother,
with your peripheral vision
you called me by some other name
as if you wanted
twice the love

swept up
into my own
Saturday night fever,
I settle for less,
I tanka my way out

I let the old woes
wail again
as if their haunting sounds
remind me—
too late, too late...

I do not leaf through
yesterday's photos
of that long trail back—
see, this monkey-face me
standing before last week's class

I've no Shiki
sickbed on the mats,
and still,
doesn't my soul
have a headache?

of late
it's the elderly sick
I visit—
when will I visit
myself?

#2

Moby Dick
tanka

Ahab,
like some forger
of Shakespearean lines,
you mouth even a harpoon-fist
into words

lift me,
muse,
into Ahab's language,
dark peripheries
surrounded by white

Ishmael,
where did you learn
to record
as if even tanka
were meant to hurl away worlds?

to pursue
and pursue,
leg in the maw
of powers monstrous—
oh, muse, were five down ever like that?

sharks
at those oars
driving a universe
into storms—
oh, Ishmael, what you saw, what experienced!

balance me,
Ishmael,
on harpoon points,
on sea-spilled undulations,
and let that white whale drive me too

Sanford Goldstein

#3

        b

     a

      t

        t

         e

          r

           i

            n

             g   si

                     le

                      n

                      c

                      e

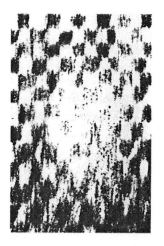

only a one-sentence
rebuke
to my kid
and all day
the lousy after-taste

the gorgeous
generosity
of my kid
tiptoeing along the edge
of tonight's roughness

thick donuts
in a brown bag:
a kid offering
to this Sunday
god of wrath

Sanford Goldstein

day of cremation
and my three tanka
waiting wordless
in that room
of Japanese mats

201

#4

b
o
d
y

                    l
              a   a
           n   u   g
              g   e

wind me up
for the toy maneuver—
marches
along corridors,
marionette nods

how this morning's
bitch
guarded its patch of lawn
and forced me
to the street

the nails age too
in spite of a mouth
full of teeth,
and even the toes
show the toil

mouth
watering
all the time:
is it sexual?
is it death?

everywhere
into the brightest shapes
or deepest cracks
I carry
the dead one's moments

no longer
will she call, will she not,
and in walks too
there's a pitted path
for a head in a battered cap

#5

kids

a

t

t

h

e

i

r

g   . . . . . s

a   e . .

m

by the creek
potatoes scrotum-black
marshmallows
impaled on a stick
and all the stories grotesque

after
the loss
a toilet-seat blues
trying to rub it
away

Sanford Goldstein

all
the games
in those days
serious
as jockstraps

the way
the wind took
that kite
infinite
the length of spring

substituting
a finger
in the basement dark
and all the giggles
hushed

prefiguration
in the games
kids play:
Dostoyevsky
and his square yard of space

on the fall
scavenger list
one four-leaf clover:
how I bruised
all crawling things!

#6

```
              s
       u
          b
          s
             t
          i
       t




                 u

                 t

                   i

                   o

                   n




                      s
```

tonight's relief:
pie
deep
in a cafeteria
booth

       trying
       to burn up
       calories
       and something else
       this June day

the handle
of this racket,
these green
balls,
and this celibate me!

no one will dance
for the dead
on this American street—
I remember Japanese hands,
Japanese legs long as cranes

sweet to me
this solitude
when I link chain
to door
and shut out the rough world

womb-safe
under Japanese counterpanes—
outside
a white wind
that means business

#7

t

a

n

k   a

g
y
r
a
t

i
o
n

s

even in this battered
toasted cheese
squeezed into my bag,
I find the music
of white stoves, burned pans

I listen
to the simplifications and divisions
and endless desires
weaving like brushstroke:
tonight this tanka world

my output of poems
lessened day by day,
reduced by life-length,
and still, still,
how wide my tanka world!

Sanford Goldstein

I never carried
a mirror placed Toulouse-like
in my battered cap—
and still from my tanka brush
this cascade of *me!* and *my!* and *mine!*

it's on paper
I live my other life,
the life
that has no causes to uphold,
no core to suck

drawn to you
womb-like
tonight
and tomorrow and beyond,
my tanka world!

for forty years
like an Israelite
in a scorching desert
waiting for poems
to fall in manna-relief

#...8   #...8   #...8

s
t
a
c
c
a
t
o

a
l
l
u
s
i
o
n
s

Akiko,
when you spoke
to those young men
about love ages ago,
did it include this old-fart me?

that pressure point
in my skull
is Van Gogh's whirling flowers,
is Mokichi's yellow tears,
is Takuboku's cough lonely as wind roar

Emily, at your desk
in your quiet room,
did you explode with joy
hitting with dashes
just the right catharsis?

again, Hamlet,
you haul me to your heart,
to your precious mouth,
and I feel even tanka
can scale the spectacular

whirling
in the glitter of Gatsby,
I recall
all the glory, all the ruin,
of my splintered visions

too late, too late—
is that Jamesian cry
now echoing
even in this coffee cup,
even in this scrawl down a page?

Anne Frank,
how you scribbled,
endured,
and now I tramp up these stairs
they hurried you down

#
9

t
h
i
s

s
t
u
m
p
e
d

sel
f

Sanford Goldstein

is it my own face
in tonight's square mirror,
or is it Akebono's sumo frown,
sweat over serious eyes
in his slow walk down the aisle of defeat?

I kept by the shallow water
where I could wade in safety,
and that's the image I'm left with,
the image of one who failed to leap,
who failed to plunge in and through

alone
at a table
in this huge mall,
and I feel, feel,
the size of my life

were all those years
a repeated cliché
of all I Zen-master learned,
of all I kept like a fisted glove
unable to grip itself?

on a bus
or boot-deep along some narrow street
or even as I launder
and fold shirts and socks and briefs,
mother, my mother, is dead

how this mirror-image
belies what I parade in my head
or in my legs
on my eight-mile rapid walk-trek
in June's heat or autumn's shade

I have sailed
on ephemeral seas
where some constant
anti-ephemeral thought huddles:
the sick-one won't be me

Sanford Goldstein

I have coin-tossed
my life—sometimes heads,
sometimes tails—
in cracks on sidewalks or on pinched graffiti squares,
and I am waiting even now for solid thrusts

at the end
of my white string
a soulmate came,
so close to the edge
I could not scissor it away

some
after-
thoughts

And so *This Tanka Whirl* . . . I have always felt that Takuboku was right when he said in one of his essays that tanka is a diary of the emotional life of the poet. Throughout the years I have followed this principle, yet I have myself felt that the content of traditional tanka was too restricted. Poets talk about love, about nature, about death, about friends, about frustration, about mothers and illnesses and trips. And I have done that too. But I have tried to broaden even more the content of tanka—the games of children, the impossibility of the tanka form itself, the connection of tanka to literature, my Zen experience and tanka, a multiple diversity. At the same time I have tried to remember that "tanka" in Japanese means "short song." The melody of tanka, its music, goes beyond that of the traditional pattern of 5-7-5-7-7. It has always seemed strange to me that when a Japanese recites a tanka or recalls it from memory, the words come out rapidly in the monotony of regulation time. Yet when I once heard Akiko Yosano read some of her poems on a tape someone gave me, her voice soared, and the rhythmic sound was actually like singing. I have tried to walk through my tanka world with the awareness of music, the varied tanka world having a varied music—staccato or soaring or bleak or contrapuntal. And so *This Tanka Whirl.*

—Sanford Goldstein

"two small trees by a stream in moonlight"
Etching by Kazuaki Wakui, used on the cover of
This Tanka Whirl, 2001 Clinging Vine Press edition.

Four Decades on My Tanka Road

Part VI

Encounters in This Penny World

2005

Sanford Goldstein

childhood

how we pulled
those dandelions off the hill,
one, fourteen, thirty—
we spread them and tied thin strings,
our Olympic crowns knee-swirled!

Sanford Goldstein

charcoal-black
those hot bloated potatoes
deep from dug holes—
we forked their blistered skins
and salted the dripping gold

pennies we flipped,
our hopes on heads or tails
to trick the whole world:
sometimes a joy in corners,
sometimes a magic curse

luscious the donuts
in the Jewish bakery,
and ladylocks too—
his mother tells him to say "fresh
and two brown bags for the rye"

backdoors slammed
and often narrow beds
were caves of refuge—
we escaped loud kitchen noises,
red shirt stains, smells from tight lips

Four Decades on My Tanka Road

Sanford Goldstein

adolescence

the long slow crawl
of envy—eyes, shoulders, chests,
and below-waist visions:
endless nights of perpendiculars
rubbed in silence to standstill

on some corner stoop
where voices loud or plaintive
hovered by street lights,
mysteries of plunge or retreat,
cars sputtering, faces in cracks

on park benches
the old sit with their canes,
bag lunches and scarves—
never will I be like that,
and touching his crotch, he passes

images rising
as clouds shape into dream sprawl
of whirl and edge,
a pink bonnet hums a hymn,
a sweatshirt hides the temptation

they came, those young gods
with their sturdy football legs,
their basketball arms;
often they left with raucous shouts,
often with tears jersey-masked

at the gym dance
a vacant wallflower despair
floating in pink punch,
she practices unspoken words,
wipes beads off her upper lip

as if time
in the darkened room above
only his mother's,
once more he slaps the rubber ball
against the alley's brick wall

Sanford Goldstein

education

after the chapel talk
a rush of red ties, blue blazers
crowding the freshmen,
the Jesus hymn at a frat lunch,
and he recalls Friday night's wine

she fell at once
for that modest proposal
and let out a cry—
to roast Irish babies
for the starved potato-masses!

metaphysical,
lovers as stiff twin compasses,
worlds turned to coal—
on yellow sheets against his knees
his scribbled urges down the page

before the lake
he sits on a museum bench,
no calculus, no trig,
only gliding in mindless ease,
Modigliani-necked swans

all right, his mother says,
to take twenty from the jar
for the honors key;
later at the ceremony
he asks how to pronounce the Greek

a universe of books,
sans blue sky, sans red flowers,
sans forest leaf tramp,
his world a library table,
life a barricade of fingered notes

in her black gown
and tasseled cap one hand holds,
she toes the aisle;
the triumphal music saddens
what she always thought she wanted

Sanford Goldstein

marriage

in the motel room
where three red flowers light up
the narrow stand,
twice he sheds his new nightshirt,
sometimes she hears a cat's wail

as if all their love
in the tight grip of their clasped hands
on the slow walk home,
he recalls the better or worse,
she hopes her sounds will be real

nervous and sweating
transporting the crying bundle
from hospital to home,
they stand like statues at a shrine
once it's settled in the white crib

no bed of roses
or bowl of fresh cherries
and already five years:
they eat filet at a downtown club,
dance to tunes never heard before

his bowling night
and she repeats it's all right
and hurries him out;
on the way he scolds himself
for forgetting their twentieth

death comes,
something she long desired
by her own hand;
at the end no heard voices,
no mate or kids on the front steps

in the album
the dead one smiles while the kids
mimic a green ghost;
he tells his trio it's time
to get their bags, put on their masks

Sanford Goldstein

zen

the master
in black kimono sleeves,
sweeping skirt,
the back-row disciple knows
the eye cannot see itself

told
the blue mountains run about,
the neophyte waits,
mysteries deep as gorges,
tricky chopstick-contradictions

his *mu* drawn
on rough brown paper gathered
from a men's room,
the master brushes empty
one stroke after another

no brick
to stumble over
for *mu,*
he straddles his zazen pillow,
digs two palms into his crotch

a walking zazen
frantic in the hurried wake
of spun circles,
legs freedom-energized
somewhere in the deep out-there

no sweet rosebuds
to soothe the searing eye,
no treats for the tongue,
he makes his way along Zen's
labyrinthine twists, gaps, ruts

on the floor
the master plays
with the kids—
at dinner a floating silence
thicker than satori grasp

she tells her husband
satori's in sight, almost there,
and strikes her hands
as if knowing the bright marble's
in some child's finger-gripped palm

Zen, he finds,
won't let go, stays on,
lingers;
he waves farewell to the master,
the distance to Japan an inch

watching
the master's whirling whisk
in the thick green tea,
she knows the power that steeps
even the most fragile bowl

once smitten
while reading Carlyle's vigorous
Everlasting Yea,
he now feels a Zen backlash
drowning belief and disbelief

Sanford Goldstein

euphoria

week's housework done,
she perks the Kilimanjaro
and sits for Barry:
how the stream reaches down down,
fetters falling in soft swells

semester's last class
and his twenty-two students
end their stiff questions—
the moment comes like a winged bird,
like a Prometheus unbound

his blind date nervous too
and words he stumbled over
straighten out—
wine and cheese? he asks again,
and her smile buries a decade

the six-year-old
who cried into her mother's skirt,
I won't! I won't!
wobbles front stage to loud cheers
after her fist-pumping song

talking to the wall
in his small empty kitchen,
finds the words soothe—
recalling how hard that zipper was,
he laughs till he coughs in his palm

jumping rope
and breaking his record,
he keeps going—
in a corner of his eye
someone, her apron held up

a single line
in the foreign film that night
accompanies him home—
he recites it in the shower,
intones it for his prayer

whirl him,
raucous laughter, he calls out,
and let the joy last:
buttering the whole wheat slice,
he decides to toast one more

a long-ago
depression's child
he was—
ah, those fifteen-cent sundaes,
hot fudge forever spooned!

Four Decades on My Tanka Road

retirement

his fishing line
hurled out with such freedom,
such ease,
even the face of the caught fish
smiles, tail a dance of its own

his work-packed years
filed into albums of memory
for each day's bloom—
park benches under elms are thrones,
dreams drift to circles of light

an afternoon strut
along a crowd-free street
and stops for coffee,
he readies himself for macho,
for Tarzan yodels to Jane

all those working years
she waited for housecoat ease,
for chocolate thrills—
now the goal of the coming week
her short trip to blue the gray

in New York
an after-Bottino matinee,
a concert after steak,
on the midnight elevator,
a clinging pose in the mirror

the ballgame over,
no Lou Gehrig farewell speech,
no Kate Smith blessing,
he takes the late subway home,
hoping the anger's drowned in sleep

at the retirees' feast
his smileless photo taken
with the VIP—
did he erase the cynical?
did he maneuver the balding patch?

years of work
followed a bourgeois
pattern—
now in his retirement years
more of the same

once he advised
his kids about this and that,
a circle of ears;
now they insist over cokes
that he toe their fingered line

pills
have a special routine
of their own:
he juggles them in his left hand,
peanut-tosses them one by one

do I dare and dare?
his Prufrock soliloquy
up the wooden stairs;
at midnight a chamber march,
at dawn the metronome once more

on rising,
he measures coffee for one
and scrambles the eggs;
the newspaper bunched and scanned,
he readies his cap for nature

Four Decades on My Tanka Road

Sanford Goldstein

old age

that youthful
lack of esteem for elders
he once showed—
why, it's come round full-circle
in his eighth decade cane-strut!

like golf clubs
raised over fragile heads
of red tulips,
his anger in the mirror
fades on knotting the yellow

sentimental songs
at the day-care center
for the aged:
they press him to dance, to draw,
they pat his shoulder, cut his meat

long ago
Dostoyevsky's square yard
impressed him—
now the vast mall overhead
drags to a dot his cup of black

Sanford Goldstein

you can live to be
eighty, ninety, who knows!
says a friend—
at night the bird cage is covered
and she washes stains in the sink

Chaplin
in a pushed wheelchair
came as a shock;
in tonight's paper another hero
makes his alzheimer confession

on a bench
in an open space of sky
and lawn,
he surveys the world of birds
and does not find it bad

twenty years ago
the sagging neck of an actress
made him laugh;
now before his own mirror
he juggles the comparison

Sanford Goldstein

illness/death

along the corridor
where once he wheeled her,
other patients pass—
they look down, mouths screwed wordless
knowing where this cramped road leads

two trips back home
and still unable to see
his sister's grave:
over coffee he scribbles poems
to recite before her stone

his brother tells him
each day in our seventies
one hell deeper—
the stale flesh a map of pins
stabbing in multiple places

once he read
that youth never give a thought
to far-off death:
now in his cane-walk nineties
he penny-flips dawn or midnight

all these years
when aunts and cousins and friends
died like embers fading,
he skipped their crowded rites,
refused the coffin avalanche

at the final site
listening to the stark poems
of others,
he wonders if some word-maker
will offer him a thirty-one

those nights at camp
when he heard the bugle mourn
that day was done,
myriad-stars beyond his tent
foretold he would never die

skeptical of karma
and hesitant on rebirth,
he whirls to the side:
love in this anticlimax world
nirvana enough for him

told about
the book of eternal life
on New Year's day,
hears the shofar sound above,
his name blown to desert dust

sick
for the very first time
in seventy years—
curious is he to discover
the physician's twists and turns

coughing
from morning to coal-black night
over his Lucky Strikes,
he avoids her I-told-you-so,
lies poised on his caved-in back

he refused the fray,
refused the circle's finite points
and stayed safe;
now he recalls the stages
where steps faltered, staggered, slowed

a non-believer,
and still Amazing Grace
grabs him,
joy spreading through a glimpse
of hands tugging a silver cross

Sanford Goldstein

a summing up

like Maugham,
the spinster recited the prayer
once in her youth;
again at dawn her deep wound
no encounter ever healed

did all the anguish
come from that dirty moment
repeated at six?
she denies it once again
and starts the process anew

never did he want
to marry, only the sister
now gone these ten years;
he sits before the soft drink
and imagines their endless dance

not a regret,
he repeats to himself
at the end;
he practices his best smile
for the world surging ahead

his brief poems
never caught on over the years
to make a stir;
again he reads them aloud
and finds them still okay

listening
to the preacher strike the air
over endless sins,
she tries a substitute word
and lets her mind ride off

thirty years of zazen,
and satori not in sight,
he closets his pillow:
it will be there tomorrow
for his early morning routine

adventures
did not come to him
early or late;
he refused to harbor one
and went to the movies instead

to the muse
of his embittered world,
a toast:
let the harmony in at last
for someone with woeful eyes

Four Decades on My Tanka Road

afterword . . .

For more than forty years I have been connected to tanka, both as a co-translator of famous Japanese tanka poets and as a writer of my own tanka in English. Takuboku started me on this long tanka road. I wrote decades ago that once having seen some of his tanka, I felt as if my poetic world had been transformed. His was the light for me never seen on land or sea. At the same time I clung to the feeling that haiku was a nature poem and that tanka was a poem on the poet's life or thoughts or feelings. As Takuboku taught me in a 1909 essay entitled "Poems to Eat," tanka are a diary of the emotional changes in a poet's life.

In the early days I wrote tanka on napkins or scraps of paper. When I found I had written one I liked, I put it in a notebook somewhere. Eventually I started sending out poems to the short-poem magazines. The rejections were constant. Only haiku was the rage. If my poems were not haiku, no one wanted them. But I persevered, and in the seventies tanka gained a small toehold, and I found my tanka being published in the States and Canada.

Now I know that tanka is on the rise in several countries. Of course that brings pleasure to all tanka-makers.

In 1997, the Haiku Society of America made a draft definition of tanka, and in its definition the society cited a point I had made in an essay entitled "Tanka: Off the Back Burner," which had been published in *Frogpond* in 1992. I first learned about this reference in the spring 2002 Tanka Society of America Newsletter: "In the words of Sanford Goldstein, 'behind the scene is the autobiographical moment of the poet.'"

But something surprising has happened to me in *Encounters in This Penny World,* for while I follow my usual practice of mentioning nature only occasionally (though I mention it more often in this collection than in some of the others), only a few poems have "I" in them, and the "I" is from the viewpoint of the character in the tanka. In the opening poems on "childhood," I do use "we," so that must include myself, but I was thinking more about the states of mind and experiences that most children go through. For the most part I avoid the "I" that I have been so delighted or saddened or confused by these many decades.

Still, all the encounters in these poems I have either lived or observed or thought about or experienced through others. The omission of the "I" leaves, I feel, the poems more as encounters, more as dramatic interludes.

When I was a high school student, I was quite impressed with Jaques in *As You Like It.* Yes, all the world's a stage and all the men and women merely players. Each of us in this short interval on earth plays many parts, and I've tried in this collection to get into those parts and the many encounters each of us confronts in the several stages from childhood to death. The coin-flip enters our various worlds, and we confront and decide and accept or hesitate and draw back. Inevitably there is a summing up.

Sometimes I feel that critics of tanka are more obsessed with the tanka's 31 syllables (often fewer or often more) than with its content. Many of my earliest tanka might be called minimalist, and I remember translating a poem in *Tangled Hair* (#100) in which I used "We" as the only word in a single line—how the critics leaped on that one! Yet often over the years I have had tanka that reached fifty syllables or more. But two critical readers pointed out that I ought to have more syllabic control in my collection, and I realized they were right. I am grateful to them, for these dramatic encounters demand stylistic restraint.

Sanford Goldstein
Niigata, Japan 2004

Four Decades on My Tanka Road

Selective Bibliography of Works by Sanford Goldstein

Tanka Books:

This Tanka World. Goldstein, Sanford. Calligraphy by Akiko Minami. ASIN: B0006CVURE. Paperback, saddle-stitched, 5½"x8½", 53 pages. West Lafayette, IN: A PURDUE POETS COOPERATIVE BOOK distributed by Sparrow Press, 1977. Copyright © 1977 by Sanford Goldstein.

Gaijin Aesthetics. Goldstein, Sanford. No ISBN. Paperback, most saddle-stitched, some bound by thread, 5½"x8", 32 pages. (W. N. J. series number 17.) La Crosse, WI: Juniper Press, 1983. Copyright © 1983 by Sanford Goldstein.

At the Hut of the Small Mind : A Tanka Sequence. Goldstein, Sanford. ISBN 0-994676-37-5. Paperback, perfect bound, 8⅝" w x 4" h., 54 pages. Gualala, CA: AHA Books, 1992. Copyright © 1992 by Sanford Goldstein.

Records of a Well-Polished Satchel: . . . No. 7, 14 Occasion Tanka. Goldstein, Sanford. ASIN: B0006QCUDI. Paperback, saddle-stitched, 3½"x6¼", 16 pages, landscape orientation. (Chickadee Series Number 8; 175 copies) La Crosse, WI: Juniper Press, 1995. Copyright © 1995 by Sanford Goldstein.

This Tanka World of Strings. Goldstein, Sanford & Kenneth Tanemura. 28 pages. Redwood, CA: n. p., 1995. Copyright © 1995 by Sanford Goldstein & Kenneth Tanemura.

This Tanka Whirl. Goldstein, Sanford. Drawings by Kazuaki Wakui. ISBN 0-9702457-3-4. Paperback, saddle-stitched, 5½"x8½", 56 pages. Coinjock, NC: Clinging Vine Press, 2001. Copyright © 2001 by Sanford Goldstein.

Encounters in This Penny World. A tanka collection by Sanford Goldstein. Goldstein, Sanford. E.D. Blodgett, literary editor. ISBN 0-9737674-0-5. Paperback, perfect bound, 5¼" x 8⅛", 96 pages. Edmonton, AB: Inkling Press, 2005. Copyright © 2005 by Sanford Goldstein.

Edited:

Five Lines Down. [FVLD] journal. Goldstein, Sanford, & Kenneth Tanemura. eds. Redwood City, CA: 1994-1996.
— Compilation: *Five Lines Down: A Landmark in English Tanka,* compiled and edited by Denis M. Garrison. ISBN 978-0-6151-5621-7. Trade paperback, perfect bound, 6" x 9", 160 pages. Baltimore, MD, Modern English Tanka Press, 2007.

Sixty Sunflowers : Tanka Society of America Members' Anthology 2006 - 2007. Goldstein, Sanford, editor. ISBN-10: 0615152287. ISBN-13: 978-0615152288. Trade paperback, 6"x9", 108 pages, [TSAM]. Baltimore, MD: TSA & Modern English Tanka Press, 2007.

Translations:

Arishima, Takeo, *Labyrinth* (Library of Japan), Trans. Sanford Goldstein and Seishi Shinoda, ISBN-10: 0819182931. ISBN-13: 978-0819182937. Hardcover, 5.5" x 8.8", 230 pages. The Pacific Basin Institute, 1992. Madison Books, 2000.

Ibuse, Masuji, *"Salamander,"* Trans. Yokoö Sadamichi and Sanford Goldstein. *Japan Quarterly,* vol. 13, no. 1 (1966). Pp. 71-75.

Inoue, Yasushi, *The Hunting Gun* (1949), Trans. Yokoö Sadamichi and Sanford Goldstein. ISBN 0-8048-0257-2. 74 pages. Tokyo: Rutland, VT: Charles E. Tuttle,1961.

Ishikawa, Takuboku, *Romaji Diary and Sad Toys.* Trans. Sanford Goldstein and Seishi Shinoda. Tokyo: Rutland, VT: Tuttle, 1985. ISBN-10: 0804832536. ISBN-13: 978-0804832533. Trade paperback, 5.3"x7.9", 279 pages. Tokyo: Rutland, VT: Tuttle, 2000.
Ishikawa, Takuboku, *Sad Toys.* Trans. Sanford Goldstein and Seishi Shinoda. 198 pages. West Lafayette, IN: Purdue UP, 1977.

Masaoka, Shiki, *Songs from a Bamboo Village: Selected Tanka from Take no Sato Uta.* Trans. Sanford Goldstein and Seishi Shinoda. 488 pages. Tokyo: Rutland, VT: Charles E. Tuttle, 1998.

Mori, Ogai, *The Wild Geese.* Trans. Kingo Ochiai and Sanford Goldstein.

ISBN-10: 0804810702. ISBN-13: 978-0804810708. Trade paperback, 5.3"x8.1", 128 pages. Tokyo: Rutland, VT: Charles E. Tuttle, 1974.

Mori, Ogai, *The Wild Geese*. Trans. Kingo Ochiai and Sanford Goldstein. ASIN: B000LX2A0E. Trade paperback, 119 pages. Tokyo: Rutland, VT: Charles E. Tuttle, 1987.

Mori, Ogai, *Vita Sexualis* (Tuttle Classics), Trans. Sanford Goldstein and Kazuji Ninomiya. ISBN-10: 0804810486. ISBN-13: 978-0804810487. Trade paperback, 4.3"x7.2", 153 pages. Tokyo: Rutland, VT: Charles E. Tuttle, 1972.

Natsume, Sōseki, *To the Spring Equinox and Beyond* (Classics of Japanese Literature), Trans. Kingo Ochiai and Sanford Goldstein. ISBN-10: 0804833281. ISBN-13: 978-0804833288. Trade paperback, 5.1"x7.9", 336 pages. Tokyo: Rutland, VT: Charles E. Tuttle, 1985.

Ryōkan, *Ryōkan: Selected Tanka Selected Haiku*. Trans. Sanford Goldstein, Shigeo Mizuguchi, and Fujisato Kitajima. 209 pages. Niigata-shi, Japan: Kokodo, 2000.

Saitō, Mokichi, *Red Lights: Selected Tanka Sequences from Shakkō*. Trans. Seishi Shinoda and Sanford Goldstein. 385 pages. West Lafayette, IN: Purdue UP, 1989.

Setouchi, Harumi, *Beauty In Disarray*, Trans. Sanford Goldstein and Kazuji Ninomiya. ISBN-10: 0804818665 & 0804833222. ISBN-13: 978-0804833226. Trade paperback, 5.1"x7.8", 351 pages. Tokyo: Rutland, VT: Charles E. Tuttle, 1993.

Takeda, Taijun, *This Outcast Generation* and *Luminous Moss* (two novelettes), Trans. Sanford Goldstein and Yusaburo Shibuya. 145 pages. Tokyo: Rutland, VT: Charles E. Tuttle, 1967.

Yosano, Akiko, *Tangled Hair: Selected Tanka from Midaregami*. Trans. Sanford Goldstein and Seishi Shinoda. ISBN-10: 0911198261. ISBN-13: 978-0911198263. Hard cover, 165 pages. Lafayette, IN: Purdue U Studies, 1971.

Yosano, Akiko, *Tangled Hair: Selected Tanka from Midaregami*. Trans. Sanford Goldstein and Seishi Shinoda. ISBN-10: 0804815224. ISBN-13: 978-0804815222. Trade paperback, perfect-bound, 165 pages. Tokyo: Rutland, VT: Charles E. Tuttle, 1987.

Yosano, Akiko, *Tangled Hair: Selected Tanka from Midaregami.* Trans. Sanford Goldstein and Seishi Shinoda. ISBN-10: 0887273734. ISBN-13: 978-0887273735. Trade paperback, perfect-bound, 5"x7.9", 165 pages. Boston-Worcester, MA: Cheng & Tsui, 2002.

Biography

my mother:

at times, mother,
with your peripheral vision
you called me by some other name
as if you wanted
twice the love

      my wife:

      rest
      dear wife
      from no-thought
      from riddles of the universe
      from the master's command

            my children:

            thick donuts
            in a brown bag:
            a kid offering
            to this Sunday
            god of wrath

my Zen master:

his *mu* drawn
on rough brown paper gathered
from a men's room,
the master brushes empty
one stroke after another

my friend:

at the end
of my white string
a soulmate came,
so close to the edge
I could not scissor it away

my teaching:

for fifty-four years
long comments on student
compositions—
yours, Thomas Wolfe,
longer, more passionate

my spanned life:

I have used sandpaper
to smooth down
the rough edges of
forty years of pain—
I'm a gloss, I'm a précis

my poems:

drawn to you
womb-like
tonight
and tomorrow and beyond,
my tanka world!

a summing up:

I kept by the shallow water
where I could wade in safety,
and that's the image I'm left with,
the image of one who failed to leap,
who failed to plunge in and through

Recent Books from
MODERN ENGLISH TANKA PRESS

Four Decades on My Tanka Road : Tanka Collections of Sanford Goldstein
● Sanford Goldstein. Fran Witham, Ed.

this hunger, tissue-thin : new & selected tanka 1995–2005 ● Larry Kimmel

Jun Fujita, Tanka Pioneer ● Denis M. Garrison, Ed.

Landfall : Poetry of Place in Modern English Tanka
● Denis M. Garrison and Michael McClintock, Eds.

Lip Prints : Tanka and Other Short Poems 1979-2007 ● Alexis Rotella

Ouch : Senryu That Bite ● Alexis Rotella

Eavesdropping : Seasonal Haiku ● Alexis Rotella

Tanka Teachers Guide ● Denis M. Garrison, Ed.

Five Lines Down : A Landmark in English Tanka
● Denis M. Garrison, Ed.

Sixty Sunflowers: TSA Members' Anth. 2006-2007 ● Sanford Goldstein, Ed.

The Dreaming Room : Modern English Tanka in Collage and Montage Sets
● Michael McClintock and Denis M. Garrison, Eds.

Eight Shades of Blue ● Haiku by Denis M. Garrison

Haiku Harvest 2000-2006 ● Denis M. Garrison, Ed.

The Salesman's Shoes ● Tanka by James Roderick Burns

Hidden River ● Haiku by Denis M. Garrison

The Five-Hole Flute : Modern English Tanka in Sequences and Sets
● Denis M. Garrison and Michael McClintock, Eds.

www.modernenglishtankapress.com